D0772341

Millan, Dianne M., 19
adan and Id al-Fitr /

008.
05216985055
03/12/09

RAMADAN AND ID AL-FITR

REVISED AND UPDATED

Dianne M. MacMillan

Enslow Elementary

an imprint of

Enslow Publishers, Inc.

40 Industrial Road
Box 398
Berkeley Heights, NJ 07922
USA

http://www.enslow.com

Acknowledgments

The author and publisher wish to thank Dr. Frank Peters, professor of religion at New York University, Dr. Muzammil H. Siddiqi, religious director of the Islamic Society of Orange County (Calif.), and Tamim Ansary for their careful reading of the manuscript; and Dr. Aman Attieh, lecturer in Arabic languages, University of Texas, Austin, for her review of the Arabic language and pronunciations used in the text.

Enslow Elementary, an imprint of Enslow Publishers, Inc.

Enslow Elementary® is a registered trademark of Enslow Publishers, Inc.

Copyright © 2008 by Enslow Publishers, Inc.

All rights reserved.

No part of this book may be reproduced by any means without the written permission of the publisher.

Library of Congress Cataloging-in-Publication Data

MacMillan, Dianne M., 1943–
  Ramadan and Id al-Fitr, revised and updated / Dianne M. MacMillan. — Rev. and updated ed.
      p. cm. — (Best holiday books)
    Summary: "Read about the beginnings of the Ramadan and Id al-Fitr celebrations, and find out how they are celebrated in the United States"—Provided by publisher.
    Includes bibliographical references and index.
    ISBN-13: 978-0-7660-3045-9
    ISBN-10: 0-7660-3045-8
    1. Ramadan—Juvenile literature. 2. 'Id al-Fitr—Juvenile literature. 3. Fasts and feasts—Islam—Juvenile literature. I. Title.
  BP186.4.M27 2007
  297.3'6—dc22   2007002425

Printed in the United States of America

10 9 8 7 6 5 4 3 2 1

To Our Readers: We have done our best to make sure all Internet Addresses in this book were active and appropriate when we went to press. However, the author and the publisher have no control over and assume no liability for the material available on those Internet sites or on other Web sites they may link to. Any comments or suggestions can be sent by e-mail to comments@enslow.com or to the address on the back cover.

Illustration Credits: Ali Mansuri, p. 10; Artvale, p. 8; Associated Press, pp. 12, 16, 25, 28, 30, 34, 36, 38, 40, 42; © Bob Daemmrich/The Image Works, pp. 1, 41; © David Grossman/The Image Works, p. 6; Enslow Publishers, p. 23 (background); © Ilyas Dean/The Image Works, p. 37; © istockphoto.com/Damir Cudic, p. 20; © istockphoto.com/Kenneth C. Zirkel, p. 23 (book); © istockphoto.com/Shafiur Rahman, p. 32; © 2007 Jupiter Corporation, p. 4; Lawrence Migdale/Photo Researchers, Inc., p. 14; Paul Cowan/Shutterstock, 44; Peter Zaharov/Shutterstock, 18; Radomil Binek, p. 21; Shutterstock, p. 3.

Cover Photo: © Bob Daemmrich/The Image Works

Contents

BREAKFAST BEFORE DAWN

IN MANY HOMES ACROSS THE UNITED STATES, families wake up while it is still dark outside. They gather in the kitchen to eat an early morning breakfast. The table is filled with plates of delicious food. It is several hours before the children leave for school. Everyone talks and laughs. Outside, the last stars and the moon are visible. Why are these families eating so early?

This early morning breakfast is called sahur (suh-HOOR). These families believe in the religion called Islam (is-LAHM). They are getting ready for a day without food or water. This will be their last meal until sunset.

This is Ramadan (rah-mah-DAHN). It is the ninth month of the Islamic calendar. It is also a holiday that lasts almost thirty days. It is followed by a joyous festival called Id al-Fitr (EED ul-FIT-er). These special days are celebrated all over the world by people who follow the Islamic religion.

A Bangladeshi-American family in Brooklyn, New York, celebrates Id al-Fitr.

MUHAMMAD

PEOPLE WHO FOLLOW THE RELIGION OF ISLAM are called Muslims (MUS-limz). Islam is a very old religion. The word Islam means "submission to the will of God." It began with a man named Muhammad (muh-HAH-mud). Muhammad was a prophet. A prophet is a special person who tells others messages from God.

Muhammad was born in the year A.D. 570 in the city of Mecca (MEK-kah) in Arabia. Today this is in the country of Saudi

Arabia. Muhammad's parents died when he was young. He was raised by his grandfather and later on by an uncle.

The people who lived in Arabia were called Arabs. Mecca was a trade center in the desert. Long lines of camels carried goods and spices across the desert. These were called caravans. Caravans came from Egypt, Persia, and Syria. All of the trade routes passed through Mecca.

The Arab people believed in many gods and spirits. Statues and shrines were built in Mecca. People came from different places to trade and to pray before these statues.

The most important shrine was the Ka'bah (KAH-bah). It was a cubelike building with a black stone built into one corner. The Arab people believed that it was built by their ancestor Abraham many centuries before. An ancestor is a family member who is no longer living.

Muhammad grew up and became a caravan leader. When he was forty years

Muslims pray around the Ka'bah in Mecca, Saudi Arabia, in 2006.

old, he had a vision. In his vision, the angel Gabriel told him that he must preach the word of God, or Allah. The Arabic word for God is Allah (al-LAH).

For the next few years, Muhammad had many visions from the angel. Muhammad could not read or write, so he memorized the words spoken to him. Then Muhammad spoke the words exactly as he received them. Some of his followers wrote the words down. The words were gathered together to make a book called the Qur'an (ko-RAHN).

At first, only Muhammad's family believed that his messages were from God. But slowly more people began to accept his teaching. For the next twelve years, Muhammad preached to everyone that there was only one God. Muhammad told the people that they had to stop praying to the other gods. This angered the leaders of Mecca. They were afraid they might lose business if people stopped coming to pray to all the other gods. Many leaders wanted to kill Muhammad.

Finally Muhammad and his followers were forced to leave Mecca. They escaped to the city of Medina. This escape, or flight, is called the Hegira (he-JIH-rah). It took place in the year A.D. 622. This date was so important that it became the first year of the Muslim calendar.

Many people in Medina accepted Muhammad as a prophet. Muhammad felt certain that he was following the will of God. He formed an army and his power grew. In the year 630, his army of ten thousand men marched on Mecca. The people of Mecca opened their gates and accepted the new religion of Islam.

Muslims praying at night with the skyline of Mecca in the background.

Muhammad destroyed all the shrines and statues of the other gods. But he did not destroy the Ka'bah. Instead, he kissed the black stone. This became a holy place. Since that time, all Muslims face in the direction of Mecca and the Ka'bah when praying.

Muhammad died two years later at the age of sixty-two. Within one hundred years of his death, the Islamic religion had spread all across the continent. Islam stretched from the Atlantic Ocean on the west to the borders of China on the east.

Today Islam is the second largest religion in the world. There are more than 1 billion followers. In fifty-seven countries, most of the people are Muslims. Many of these countries are in the Middle East, North Africa, Central Asia, and Southeast Asia. There are more than 2.5 million Muslims in the United States and Canada.

> Today Islam is the second largest religion in the world.

A grandfather in Princeton, New Jersey, reads the Qur'an to his family members during Ramadan.

THE PILLARS OF ISLAM

THE ISLAMIC FAITH IS SIMPLE. IT IS FOUNDED on five duties, or rules. These rules are called the Pillars of Islam. Children are taught the duties as soon as they are old enough to understand.

The first rule is called the shahadah (shah-HAH-duh). This means to say and believe "There is no God but Allah and Muhammad is the Messenger of Allah." Muslims say this many times every day.

The second rule is called the salat (sah-LAHT). This means daily prayer. Muslims pray five times a day in a building called a mosque (MOSK). It is based on an old Arabic word meaning "place of kneeling." Prayers are said at dawn, at midday, at mid-afternoon, in the evening, and before bed.

Before praying, Muslims remove their shoes and wash. Muslims always face in

Muslim girls in Brooklyn, New York, take a break from studying in order to say their daily afternoon prayers.

the direction of Mecca, the holy city, when praying. Muslims in the United States and Canada always face east.

The third duty is called zakat (zuh-KAT). This means to give money to the poor. Every Muslim is called to help those who have less in any way he or she can.

The fourth rule is the fast of Ramadan. For this fast, all healthy Muslims over the age of twelve go without food or water from dawn to sunset during the month of Ramadan. Children under the age of twelve are encouraged to fast for a day several times during the month.

The fifth duty of a Muslim is to make a pilgrimage, or journey, to the city of Mecca once in his or her lifetime. People who go on the journey are called pilgrims. This pilgrimage is called the hajj (HAAJ). While on the pilgrimage, Muslims wear special clothes. They also have certain prayers and ceremonies. As many as 2 million Muslims travel to Mecca each year.

This is the famous Blue Mosque of Istanbul in the early evening.

MOSQUES, MINARETS, AND THE QUR'AN

MOSQUES ARE IMPORTANT TO MUSLIMS. Mosques usually have a high dome and at least one tower. Larger mosques have several towers. The tall tower is called a minaret (mihn-uh-REHT). Long ago, a man called a muezzin (mu-EZ-zin) would climb the tower and call the people to prayer.

The minaret of a mosque. A man would climb up the tower to call out to Muslims and tell them it was time to pray.

Today, most mosques use loudspeakers with recorded messages.

Inside the mosque is a large open room. There are no altars, furniture, or chairs. People stand and then kneel on the floor when praying. The floors are often covered with beautiful carpets. People also use prayer mats.

At one end of the building is a small alcove. This is called the mihrab (mih-RAHB). It lets people know the direction of Mecca. Everyone faces toward it. Men cover their heads as a sign of respect to God.

The person who leads the prayers is called an imam (ih-MAHM). Each prayer time lasts about ten minutes. Prayers are always said in Arabic.

Women and girls pray separately from the men and

This is the mihrab in the Hagia Sophia in Istanbul. A mihrab points to Mecca, so Muslims know which way to face when they pray.

boys when they come to the mosque. Most often the women say their prayers at home.

There is also a staircase that leads to a small platform. This is called the minbar (MIN-bar). On Fridays, Muslim men are expected to go to the mosque for midday prayers. After prayers, someone preaches from the minbar.

There can be no pictures of living things in the mosque. In this way, the believers will think only of God. But the walls and ceilings are often decorated with verses from the Qur'an. They are written in beautiful writing called calligraphy. Designs are used on tiles that also cover the walls.

Before entering a mosque, Muslims remove their shoes. They wash their hands, face, arms, and feet in a special

> The walls and ceilings of a mosque are often decorated with verses from the Qur'an.

way. Mosques have large fountains in a courtyard for the washing. Prayers are said in the same way in the mosque as they would be at home or elsewhere. At home, shoes are removed and washing is done before prayers.

It is a custom that women and girls over the age of twelve dress modestly and cover their heads when they are

The Qur'an is the Muslim holy book.

out in public. The scarves they wear around their heads and shoulders are called hijabs (hi-JAHBS). Some Muslim-American women and girls wear hijabs. Others wear them only for religious events. Others do not follow the custom at all.

The Qur'an is a holy book. All of the words that the angel Gabriel told Muhammad are written in the Qur'an. The words are in Arabic. The Qur'an has been translated into other languages as well. However, Muslims believe that if the words are not in Arabic, they do not have the same power.

For this reason, all Muslims try to learn to read Arabic. The Arabic language is read from right to left. When the Qur'an is read out loud, the words are chanted.

Muslim men and women cover their heads while reading the Qur'an. This is a sign of respect. The Qur'an cannot ever touch the ground or get dirty. Muslims keep it covered with a cloth when they are not using it.

The Qur'an has 114 chapters called suras (SOO-rahs). Muslims try to memorize as many verses as they can. This takes many years of study because there are more than six thousand verses. If someone memorizes the entire Qur'an, the person is called a hafiz (HAH-fiz).

Students in a class in Philadelphia.

The Qur'an tells Muslims how to live. It teaches them to be kind and loving.

The family has a huge party to celebrate.

Children learn to read the Qur'an. In the United States, Muslim children may attend an Islamic school. They learn about their religion and other school subjects. Others go to Saturday school held at a mosque or at an Islamic center. They learn to read and write Arabic. Most mosques have Qur'an schools for adults and children.

The Qur'an tells Muslims how to live. It teaches Muslims to be kind and loving. It tells them to trust in God at all times. The Qur'an has some of the same stories found in the Old and New Testaments of the Bible. There are stories about Adam, Noah, Abraham, Moses, and Jesus. Some Muslims carry a copy of the Qur'an with them wherever they go.

RAMADAN

Muslims look forward to Ramadan. The Islamic calendar is based on the moon. The Muslim day begins at sunset, and each new month begins with the appearance of a new moon. Each month is twenty–nine or thirty days long. The lunar year is 354 days. That means that the Muslim year is ten to eleven days shorter than the solar year. Ramadan is always the ninth month of the Islamic calendar. But the date for Ramadan changes every year. It can occur in any season.

A man looks at the sky just after sunset to find the new moon that shows the start of Ramadan.

In Muslim countries, people wait with excitement for the first sight of the new moon that begins Ramadan. They climb rooftops or hills or go out into the desert. As soon as the moon is seen, people share good wishes with one another. Children greet their parents and grandparents. They kiss their hands as a sign of respect. The families go home to prepare for prayers and the early morning meal.

In other countries, the news of the moon is broadcast on radio and television. In olden days, people fired a cannon when the moon was seen.

People who are very old or sick or mothers who are nursing babies do not have to fast. But they must fast at some other time when they are able. If they cannot fast, they are asked to feed a poor person instead.

Muslims fast because they believe that God asked them to do so. By fasting, they feel they become stronger in their faith. They also learn how poor people feel when they do not have enough food to eat.

Each morning, the family rises early. They eat their breakfast, or sahur. If Ramadan falls in the winter when days are shorter, the meal will be light. If Ramadan is in summertime and there are many hours before sunset, then the

Families at a mosque in Cedar Rapids, Iowa, end their day of fasting during Ramadan.

meal will be much larger. After breakfast, the family gets ready for prayers either at home or at the mosque.

At sunset, Muslims break their fast with a glass of water or by eating a few dates. This is what the prophet Muhammad did. Everyone leaves the table to pray. When prayers are over, they return to enjoy a wonderful meal. The meal at sunset is called iftar (if-TAHR). Different foods are cooked at home or bought at a store.

Long ago, people would listen for the call from the minaret of the mosque to know when it was sunset. Today, in large cities in the United States, the official time is announced on the radio or television. The time of sunset is also listed in newspapers. In other areas, people telephone the mosque or Islamic center.

Muslims try to read the Qur'an from start to finish at least once during Ramadan. They spend more time in prayer. They try hard not to quarrel or

This is a typical breakfast for a family in Bangladesh during Ramadan.

use mean words. Everyone tries to be cheerful and kind.

During Ramadan, there are few activities planned during the day. In Muslim countries, restaurants are closed. Everyone waits until evening. When night arrives, mosques are lit, and restaurants and amusement parks are open. There is visiting and shopping.

> The twenty-seventh night of Ramadan is called the Night of Power.

The twenty-seventh night of Ramadan is called the Night of Power. Muslims believe that this is when the Qur'an was first given to Muhammad. Because they are not completely sure of the exact night, some Muslims spend the last ten nights of Ramadan in prayer.

Many Muslims believe that the last ten nights of Ramadan are holy. They believe that during these nights angels come down to earth and bless everyone.

An imam preaches at the Islamic Center in Paterson, New Jersey.

PREPARING FOR ID AL-FITR

ID IS AN ARABIC WORD. IT MEANS "A FESTIVAL OF happiness and a time of great joy." Id al-Fitr marks the end of the fast of Ramadan. During the last week of Ramadan, people prepare for Id al-Fitr. Cards are sent to neighbors, friends, and relatives.

Muslims give to the poor all during the year. But they are asked to give even more during Ramadan. The money is collected

Muslim girls admire a display of decorative lights at a night bazaar in Singapore during Ramadan.

and given away a few days before Id. In this way, poor families have money to buy gifts and food for the celebration. Rich Muslim countries collect money and send it to the poorer Muslim countries.

Children grow more excited as the month of Ramadan draws to a close. They try to guess what gifts they will receive. Will there be new clothes, shoes, or toys? But one gift is certain. They will receive lots of candy. Everyone gives candy of all kinds to the children.

Adults also look forward to the new clothes and celebrations. Houses are cleaned and painted. Then they are decorated with flowers and banners. The mosques are also decorated with flowers. The thirty days of Ramadan are almost over.

These Muslims are celebrating Id al-Fitr in Karachi, Pakistan.

Members of the East Texas Islamic community celebrate during Id al-Fitr.

ID AL-FITR

ID AL-FITR MARKS THE END OF THE FAST OF Ramadan. It is celebrated on the first day of the tenth month. The celebrations begin as soon as the new moon is sighted. Children and adults greet their elders by kissing their hands. Then they rush to congratulate one another.

On the morning of Id al-Fitr, Muslims wake up early. They take showers or baths and put on their best clothes. Many wear perfume. They have breakfast. Then they go to prayers. Prayers are held in large open spaces like parks and playgrounds. The whole Islamic community comes together. Women and children are also encouraged to come to prayers.

Special prayers of thanksgiving are said. Muslims thank God for giving them the month of Ramadan. They thank God for their faith and for giving them the Qur'an.

Muslims pray before the start of the 2002 Muslim Day Parade in New York City.

Camels are on display at this 2005 Id al-Fitr celebration in Austin, Texas.

Children in Qatar in the Middle East wear traditional outfits and go from house to house singing and collecting sweets during Ramadan.

When prayers are over, men, women, and children hug one another. Everyone says "Id Mubarak" (EED moo-BAH-rek), which means "Happy Id." The children receive clothes, toys, and candy.

In the United States, many Muslim communities have Id carnivals. There are rides and games for the children. Big balloons with the words "Happy Id" float everywhere. Adults greet one another by saying, "May Allah accept your prayers and fast of Ramadan."

The day is filled with visiting. Many families leave their doors open. People go from house to house visiting. In each home, they hug and congratulate one another on the fast of Ramadan. Trays of candy and sweets are on the tables for the guests.

Id is a time to forgive one another. Family members who live far away try

Many communities in the United States have Id carnivals with rides and games.

to come home for this celebration. In Muslim countries, the Id festival lasts for three days. It is a national holiday. In the United States and Canada, Muslims take a day off from work. Their children are allowed to miss a day of school.

These are some traditional Ramadan sweets from the Middle East.

Everywhere there is laughter, celebrating, and good food. There are many meat and rice dishes cooked with spices and sweets. Each family prepares their favorite foods.

As the celebration ends, Muslims from all over the world are united in their faith. They have celebrated Ramadan just as Muhammad taught. With Id al-Fitr, they have shared food, laughter, and joy. Everyone looks forward to the next Islamic holiday.

44

Allah—The Arabic word for God.

Arabic—The language of Arab people, whose ancestors lived in Arabia.

calligraphy—The art of beautiful writing.

fast—To go without food or water for a certain period of time.

hafiz—A person who has memorized the entire Qur'an.

hajj—The pilgrimage to Mecca that each Muslim must make at least once in his or her lifetime if he or she is in good health and can afford it.

Hegira—Muhammad's flight, or escape, from Mecca to Medina in the year A.D. 622.

hijab—The scarf that some Muslim women and girls wear that covers their head and shoulders.

Id al-Fitr—The festival following the fast of Ramadan. It begins on the first day of the tenth month.

iftar—The evening meal eaten after a day of fasting during Ramadan.

imam—The person who leads the prayers in the mosque.

Ka'bah—The cubelike building in Mecca that Muslims face toward when praying.

mihrab—The alcove in the mosque that shows the direction of Mecca.

minaret—A tower on the mosque from which Muslims are called to prayer.

minbar—A small platform or pulpit in the mosque where someone preaches on Fridays.

mosque—The building where Muslims come to pray and meet with other Muslims.

muezzin—The person who calls the people to prayer from the minaret.

Muslims—People who follow the religion of Islam.

pilgrimage—A long journey to a holy place. Muslims must make the pilgrimage to Mecca at least once, if they are able to.

prophet—A special person who tells others messages from God.

Qur'an—The Muslim holy book believed to be the actual words of Allah revealed to Muhammad.

Ramadan—The ninth month of the Islamic calendar.

sahur—The breakfast eaten before dawn during the month of Ramadan.

salat—The duty of all Muslims to pray five times a day.

shahadah—The reciting of the creed or belief of Islam.

sura—A chapter in the Qur'an.

zakat—The duty of all Muslims to give money to the poor.

LEARN MORE

Books

Douglass, Susan. *Ramadan*. Minneapolis: Carolrhoda Books, 2004.

Hughes, Monica. *My Id al-Fitr*. Chicago, Il.: Raintree, 2004.

Sievert, Terri. *Ramadan: Islamic Holy Month*. Mankato, Minn.: Capstone Press, 2006.

Web Sites

Islam (Muslim) for Kids
http://woodlands-junior.kent.sch.uk/Homework/religion/Islam.htm#top

Ramadan and Hari Raya Puasa for Kids and Teachers
http://www.kiddyhouse.com/Ramadan/

Ramadankids.com
http://www.ramadankids.com/index.html

INDEX